OKLAHOMA
SOONERS

BY
MARGARET WEBER

INSIDE
COLLEGE
FOOTBALL

www.av2books.com

AV² provides enriched content that supplements and complements this book. Weigl's AV² books strive to create inspired learning and engage young minds in a total learning experience.

Your AV² Media Enhanced books come alive with...

Audio
Listen to sections of the book read aloud.

Key Words
Study vocabulary, and complete a matching word activity.

Video
Watch informative video clips.

Quizzes
Test your knowledge.

Embedded Weblinks
Gain additional information for research.

Slideshow
View images and captions, and prepare a presentation.

Try This!
Complete activities and hands-on experiments.

... and much, much more!

Go to www.av2books.com, and enter this book's unique code.

BOOK CODE

AVB26889

AV² by Weigl brings you media enhanced books that support active learning.

Published by AV² by Weigl
350 5th Avenue, 59th Floor
New York, NY 10118
Website: www.av2books.com

Library of Congress Control Number: 2018968209

ISBN 978-1-7911-0078-0 (hardcover)
ISBN 978-1-7911-0079-7 (multi-user eBook)
ISBN 978-1-7911-0080-3 (single-user eBook)

Printed in Guangzhou, China
1 2 3 4 5 6 7 8 9 0   23 22 21 20 19

042019
102318

Project Coordinator: Jared Siemens   Designer: Terry Paulhus

Every reasonable effort has been made to trace ownership and to obtain permission to reprint copyright material. The publishers would be pleased to have any errors or omissions brought to their attention so that they may be corrected in subsequent printings.

The publisher acknowledges Alamy, Getty Images, Newscom and Wikimedia Commons as its primary image suppliers for this title.

INSIDE
COLLEGE
FOOTBALL

Oklahoma Sooners

CONTENTS

AV² Book Code 2
Introduction 4
History 6
The Stadium 8
Where They Play........................10
The Uniforms.............................12
Student Athletes 14
Bowl Games 16
The Coaches 18
The Mascot.................................20
Legends of the Past 22
All-Time Records 24
Timeline......................................26
Write a Biography 28
Trivia Time 30
Key Words/Index........................ 31
www.av2books.com....................32

Introduction

When the Oklahoma Sooners first took the field in 1895, they did so in the **Territory** of Oklahoma. Oklahoma did not become a state until 12 years after Sooners football began. This early beginning included players who were not students. However, it was the foundation of one of the most competitive college football teams in the United States.

Today, the Oklahoma Sooners are known as a winning team. This was not always the case. In the 1960s, the Oklahoma Sooners struggled to end each season with a winning record. They had a hard time **recruiting** talented players. These struggles continued as the Sooners looked for a coach to turn around the team's prospects.

Oklahoma defensive end Kenneth Mann logged a career total of 81 tackles and five quarterback sacks during his time as a Sooner.

Finally, in the late 1960s, the Sooners began to have seasons with winning records. Between 1970 and 1979, they won 103 games, with a win ratio of 88 percent. This decade of winning set the stage for the Sooners to become the team they are today.

Sooners quarterback Kyler Murray completed 260 passes and passed for 4,361 yards during the 2018 season.

OKLAHOMA

Stadium Gaylord Family Oklahoma Memorial Stadium

Division Division I Football Bowl Subdivision, Big 12 Conference

Head Coach Lincoln Riley

Location Norman, Oklahoma

National Championships 6

Nicknames OU, Oklahoma, Sooners

4
Number-One Overall NFL Draft Picks

22
Team Coaches

63
Former Sooners Players Who Made Super Bowl Appearances

31
Super Bowls That Included Former Sooners Players

History

The Sooners have had more **single-game victories** than any other team in the National Collegiate Athletic Association (NCAA) since **1946**.

During his three years as a member of Oklahoma's varsity team, wide receiver Tommy McDonald never played in a losing game.

The history of the Oklahoma Sooners is closely tied to the history of the United States. Sooners was a name given to early **settlers** in the Territory of Oklahoma. These settlers rushed to claim land in the territory within the time set by the government. In 1908, the University of Oklahoma football team adopted the name in honor of the determined spirit of these early settlers.

The Sooners have been playing college football for 124 years. Since the team has existed nearly as long as the sport itself, it has seen many changes. The team's first non-player coach, Vernon Parrington, was from Harvard University. He brought knowledge of the game from the East Coast, where it was starting to gain popularity. Since then, the Sooners have played in six different conferences.

The Sooners also have long-standing **rivalries**. The University of Oklahoma began in 1890, and college football began shortly after that. In 1904, the Sooners played against Oklahoma State University. This began the rivalry known as the Bedlam Series. The Bedlam Series is very popular among fans. It has also spread to other sports between the two universities. Today, the Sooners lead the series between the football teams, with 87 wins.

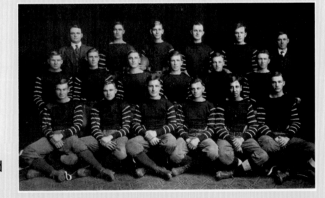

The 1915 Sooners were undefeated and outscored their opponents 370–54.

The Stadium

Before permanent lights were installed at Gaylord Family Oklahoma Memorial Stadium, the university leased portable lights so that games could be televised.

Rising out of the flat **landscape** of Oklahoma is Gaylord Family Oklahoma Memorial Stadium. It is the largest sports facility in the state, marking Oklahoma's commitment to college football. It is also one of the 15 largest college sports stadiums in the country. In addition to hosting football games, it can be used for other major events, such as concerts.

The stadium is named in part to honor Oklahoma service members. The word "memorial" recognizes all Oklahomans who were a part of the armed forces of the United States. It is also named for generous donations the university has received. Christy Gaylord Everest donated the money as part of her family's long tradition of giving to the University of Oklahoma. This donation helped fund the stadium's expansion in 2002.

Since 2000, there have been many improvements to the stadium. Every seat was replaced in 2002. There were also changes made to the scoreboards, entrances, and athletic offices. Currently, there are more plans to increase seating capacity and **renovate** the players' training rooms. The stadium's record attendance was 88,308.

Gaylord Family Oklahoma Memorial Stadium was originally named Owen Field after Sooners coach Bennie Owen, who helped raise money to build a permanent stadium. The field of play is still known as Owen Field.

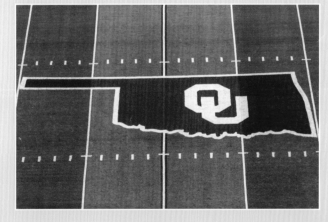

Where They Play

T he Oklahoma Sooners play home games at Gaylord Family Oklahoma Memorial Stadium. The front entrance of the stadium has large arched glass doors and cathedral-like windows. Seats surround the playing field on all sides. More than 86,000 fans can cheer on the Sooners every home game during football season.

Arena
Gaylord Family Oklahoma Memorial Stadium

Location
Norman, Oklahoma

Broke Ground
1922

Completed
1923

Surface
Real Grass

Features
- Completed a $160-million renovation in 2016
- Home to the Barry Switzer Center, a museum of Sooners history
- Has the second-largest video board among college stadiums in the country

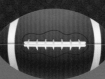

BIG 12

1 **Baylor University**
Waco, Texas

2 **Iowa State University**
Ames, Iowa

3 **Kansas State University**
Manhattan, Kansas

4 **Oklahoma State University**
Stillwater, Oklahoma

5 **Texas Christian University**
Fort Worth, Texas

6 **Texas Tech University**
Lubbock, Texas

7 **University of Kansas**
Lawrence, Kansas

☆ 8 **University of Oklahoma**
Norman, Oklahoma

9 **University of Texas at Austin**
Austin, Texas

10 **West Virginia University**
Morgantown, West Virginia

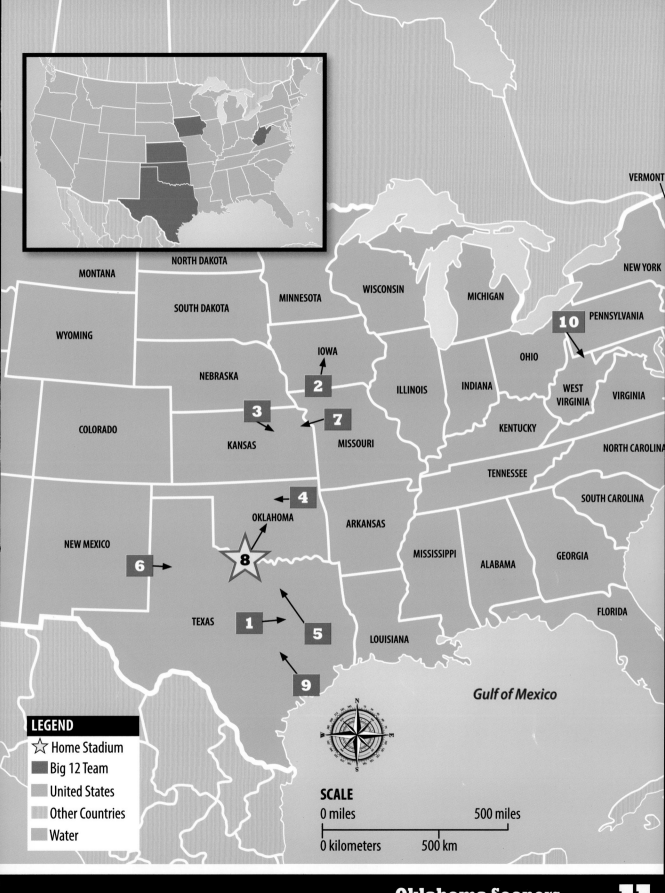

LEGEND

☆ Home Stadium

■ Big 12 Team

■ United States

■ Other Countries

■ Water

SCALE

0 miles   500 miles

0 kilometers   500 km

The Uniforms

In 1966, Oklahoma added their distinctive **OU logo** to players' helmets.

A 2018 switch to Nike's Jordan Brand uniforms included an update to the font used on the uniforms and helmets, which had not been altered since the mid-1990s.

Oklahoma's colors are crimson and cream. These colors are very important to the team and fans. They are part of the team's history, even though the uniforms have changed over time. The Sooners' very first uniform was crimson. It had cream-colored numbers. The first helmets that players wore were white.

HOME

One aspect that has changed is the word "SOONERS" across the front of the jersey. This has not always been a feature of the uniform, but has recently become more common. This helps identify Sooners players. Today, the Sooners' uniforms are white with crimson lettering, the opposite of when the team began. Improvements to the uniforms continue to be made as the sport changes. The helmets of today have an improved faceplate to protect players. In 2000, the helmets received a metallic crimson finish, a change that can make the helmets look new without straying from the crimson and cream colors the fans know and love.

AWAY

Before 1966, when the Sooners' helmets took on their current look, OU's helmet was plain white with a red stripe down the center.

Student Athletes

Oklahoma Sooners have been awarded Academic All-American prizes 30 times.

Being a college student athlete is hard work. Student athletes have to perform well on the football field and in the classroom. University of Oklahoma student athletes are required to meet a minimum grade point average. The University of Oklahoma strives to recognize players' academic achievements. In 2018, the university celebrated the 20th anniversary of its Scholar-Athlete Breakfast to honor those players who excel on the field and in the classroom.

Many student athletes are given athletic scholarships. An athletic scholarship is a financial aid agreement between the athlete and the college or university. Athletes who do not receive an athletic scholarship can be "walk-on" members of the team. This means they are on the team, but without athletic financial aid. The most famous Sooner to play as a walk-on is current National Football League (NFL) player Baker Mayfield. The University of Oklahoma awards the maximum number of football scholarships allowed, which is 85.

Football players at the University of Oklahoma must be full-time students and work toward earning a degree in order to maintain their place on the team.

Bowl Games

Coach Bob Stoops took his team to bowl games in every one of his **18 years** as coach.

The Sooners crushed their in-state rivals, the Oklahoma State Cowboys, to reach the 2015 Orange Bowl. The Clemson Tigers defeated the Sooners 37–17 in the New Year's Eve game.

After the college football season ends, a rare sports tradition begins. There is no NCAA-sponsored **postseason** for the sport of football. Instead, a variety of games called bowl games are played. There are currently 40 bowl games played between college football teams. These games give teams the chance to play rivals or new teams. It is also a chance to compete for respect and wins even after they have finished with the regular season.

The Oklahoma Sooners have competed in bowl games since 1939. Their first was the Orange Bowl, which remains the bowl where they have made the most appearances. They have played in 52 bowl games, and have won 29. Opponents vary depending on the year, but the Sooners have played Florida State University four times, which is more than any other team. Each year, bowl games offer opportunities for Sooners fans to cheer for their team outside of Oklahoma.

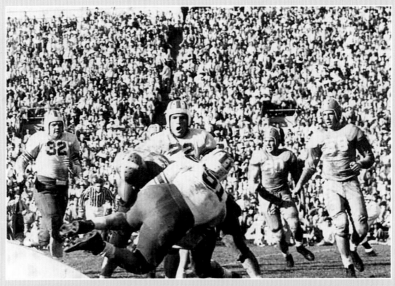

The Sooners have played in the Orange Bowl 19 times. Their first Orange Bowl appearance ended in a scoreless loss to the University of Tennessee.

The Coaches

John A. Harts only coached **one game**, in 1895, and since the Sooners lost the game, his record is **.000**.

When the University of Oklahoma hired Lincoln Riley to replace Bob Stoops, Riley was the youngest head football coach in the United States, at just 33 years old.

The Oklahoma Sooners have had a total of 22 coaches. Some of these coaches are celebrated. Others left after coaching only a single game. Only nine coaches have led the Sooners to postseason bowl games. Each coach comes to Oklahoma hoping to make his mark in Sooners history. Some of Oklahoma's most memorable coaches have high win percentages, conference titles, and even National Championships under their belts.

BARRY SWITZER Barry Switzer was the Oklahoma Sooners head coach from 1973 to 1988. He had previously been the team's **offensive coordinator**, where he excelled at a new style of offense. As head coach, Switzer won the Big Eight Conference eight years in a row, from 1973 to 1980. He also saw 54 of his players named All-Americans, and one receive a **Heisman Memorial Trophy**.

BOB STOOPS During his first season with Oklahoma in 1999, Bob Stoops won seven games. It was the first of many winning seasons he would enjoy with the Sooners. When he retired in 2017, he held the record in wins, with a total of 190. During his 18 years as coach, the Sooners won the National Championship, played in 18-straight bowl games, and produced two Heisman Trophy winners.

LINCOLN RILEY Current head coach Lincoln Riley served as the offensive coordinator under Bob Stoops from 2015 to 2017. In his first year as head coach, he was able to bring his team to the Big 12 Championship and the 2018 Rose Bowl. While Riley may be younger than most coaches, he has already proven his worth to the Sooners with 24 out of 27 overall wins.

The Mascot

The Sooner Schooner has been the official mascot of the University of Oklahoma since 1980. It is maintained and driven by OU's all-male spirit squad, the RUF/NEKS.

The first Oklahoma mascot was a dog named Mex. The dog's owner, a former U.S. Army medic named Mott Keys, found Mex while on duty in Texas during the Mexican Revolution. When Keys enrolled at OU, he brought Mex along. The dog became a mascot at games and wore a red sweater with an "O" on the side. Mex served as mascot from 1915 to 1928.

The official mascot of the Oklahoma Sooners is the Sooner Schooner. A schooner is a covered wagon. It is the type of wagon that brought settlers west during the time when Oklahoma was settled. The Sooner Schooner debuted in 1964 and became the official mascot in 1980. It is pulled by two live white horses named Boomer and Sooner.

Until 2005, there were no mascots in costume on the sidelines of Sooners football games. This changed with the introduction of two costumed horses in crimson and cream uniforms. Like the live horses, they are also named Boomer and Sooner. They cheer for the team and interact with fans. They also take photos with students and welcome everyone to the stadium on game days.

Costumed versions of Boomer and Sooner are identical except for their eye color.

Legends of the Past

For many players, their time with the Sooners is the start of a promising football career. These are some of the best-known football players to play for the University of Oklahoma.

Gerald McCoy

Gerald McCoy started all 40 games he played for Oklahoma. In 2007, McCoy was named Defensive Freshman of the Year in the Big 12 Conference. The following year, he finished the season with an interception, 30 tackles, and 6.5 sacks. He was named the Big 12 Defensive Player of the Year. McCoy was also recognized as an All-American during his final two seasons at Oklahoma. Over three seasons as a Sooner, McCoy logged 51 tackles and 14.5 sacks. He was drafted in 2009 by the Tampa Bay Buccaneers, where he plays as a defensive tackle.

Position: Defensive Tackle
Seasons: 2007–2009 (Oklahoma Sooners), 2010–Present (Tampa Bay Buccaneers)
Born: February 25, 1988, Oklahoma City, Oklahoma

Baker Mayfield

Baker Mayfield joined the Oklahoma Sooners in 2014. As a transfer student, Mayfield was able to walk on to the team and soon earned the starting quarterback position. After this accomplishment, he was offered a scholarship in order to remain with the team. In 2015, he was the *Sporting News* Player of the Year. He led his team to many victories. As a result, he earned the Heisman Trophy in 2017 with the third-highest percentage of votes in history. He was the first overall NFL **draft** pick in 2018. Today he plays for the Cleveland Browns.

Position: Quarterback
Seasons: 2015–2017 (Oklahoma Sooners), 2018–Present (Cleveland Browns)
Born: April 14, 1995, Austin, Texas

Lane Johnson

Lane Johnson began his college football career at Kilgore College in 2008. After a year, he transferred to the University of Oklahoma. As a Sooner, he played multiple positions, including offensive tackle, right tackle, and left tackle. Johnson was named an All-American in his senior year. During his senior year, he started 11 out of 13 games. In 2013, Johnson was chosen fourth overall in the NFL draft by the Philadelphia Eagles, where he is currently an offensive tackle.

Position: Offensive Tackle
Seasons: 2009–2012 (Oklahoma Sooners),
   2013–Present (Philadelphia Eagles)
Born: May 8, 1990, Cleveland, Texas

Sam Bradford

In the 2008 season, Sam Bradford logged one of the best seasons ever by a quarterback. Bradford passed for 4,720 yards with 50 touchdowns. He also led the Sooners to break two points records and win a third consecutive Big 12 Championship. Bradford became the fifth Sooner and only the second sophomore player ever to win the Heisman Trophy. Although a shoulder injury shortened his final season at Oklahoma, Bradford entered the 2009 NFL draft. He currently plays for the Arizona Cardinals.

Position: Quarterback
Seasons: 2006–2009 (Oklahoma Sooners),
 2010–2014 (St. Louis Rams),
 2015 (Philadelphia Eagles),
 2016–2017 (Minnesota Vikings),
 2018–Present (Arizona Cardinals)
Born: November 8, 1987, Oklahoma City, Oklahoma

All-Time Records

716
Points in a Season
The Sooners scored 716 points in 2008, an all-time OU record.

16,646
Most Yards Passed
Landry Jones set a Sooners career passing record of 16,646 yards between 2008 and 2012.

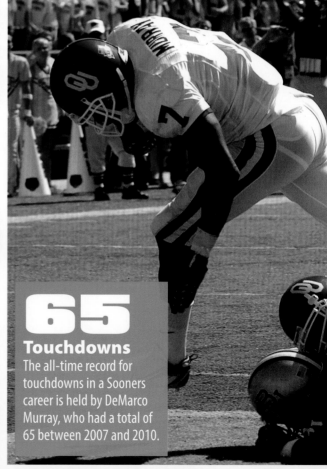

65
Touchdowns
The all-time record for touchdowns in a Sooners career is held by DeMarco Murray, who had a total of 65 between 2007 and 2010.

598
Single-Game Passing Yards
Baker Mayfield set the Sooners record for passing yards in a single game in 2017 against Oklahoma State with 598 yards.

78
Longest Punt in a Bowl Game
The longest punt by a Sooner in a bowl game was 78 yards by Scott Blanton in the 1993 John Hancock Bowl.

Timeline

Throughout the team's history, the Oklahoma Sooners have had many memorable events that have become defining moments for the team and its fans.

1895
The first game of Sooners football ever played takes place.

1953
The Sooners' 47-game winning streak begins.

1900   **1920**   **1940**   **1960**

Oklahoma becomes a state in 1907.

1923
The first game is played at Gaylord Family Oklahoma Memorial Stadium.

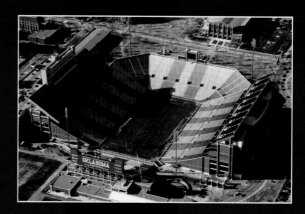

2008
Oklahoma has the highest-scoring season in all of college football history, with 343 total points.

The Future
It is an exciting time to follow Sooners football. Recent wins and NFL-bound players have made Oklahoma a popular team for fans and players alike. Coach Riley has big shoes to fill, but is looking to make his mark on the team. By carrying on the legacy of Bob Stoops, the Sooners will continue to win and bring championships home to the University of Oklahoma.

1980

2000

2020

In 1987, fans enjoy the first-ever night game played in Oklahoma football.

2013
Bob Stoops becomes the winningest coach in OU history.

2010
Three Sooners players are selected numbers 1, 3, and 4 in the NFL draft.

Write a Biography

Life Story

A person's life story can be the subject of a book. This kind of book is called a biography. Biographies often describe the lives of people who have achieved great success. These people may be alive today, or they may have lived many years ago. Reading a biography can help you learn more about a great person.

Get the Facts

Use this book, and research in the library and on the internet, to find out more about your favorite player. Learn as much about him as you can. What position does he play? What are his statistics in important categories? Has he set any records? Also, be sure to write down key events in the person's life. What was his childhood like? What has he accomplished off the field? Is there anything else that makes this person special or unusual?

Use the Concept Web

A concept web is a useful research tool. Read the questions in the concept web on the following page. Answer the questions in your notebook. Your answers will help you write a biography.

Concept Web

Adulthood
- Where does this individual currently reside?
- Does he have a family?

Your Opinion
- What did you learn from the books you read in your research?
- Would you suggest these books to others?
- Was anything missing from these books?

Childhood
- Where and when was this person born?
- Describe his parents, siblings, and friends.
- Did he grow up in unusual circumstances?

Accomplishments off the Field
- What is this person's life's work?
- Has he received awards or recognition for accomplishments?
- How have this person's accomplishments served others?

Write a Biography

Help and Obstacles
- Did this individual have a positive attitude?
- Did he receive help from others?
- Did this person have a mentor?
- Did this person face any hardships?
- If so, how were the hardships overcome?

Accomplishments on the Field
- What records does he hold?
- What key games and plays have defined his career?
- What are his stats in categories important to his position?

Work and Preparation
- What was this person's education?
- What was his work experience?
- How does this person work?
- What is the process he uses?

Trivia Time

Take this quiz to test your knowledge of the Oklahoma Sooners.
The answers are printed upside down under each question.

1 In what year did the Sooners' 47-game winning streak begin?

A. 1953

2 What color are the current helmets for the Sooners?

A. Crimson

3 In what year did Sooners football begin?

A. 1895

4 What is the name of the Sooners' stadium?

A. Gaylord Family Oklahoma Memorial Stadium

5 How many bowl appearances have the Sooners made?

A. 52

6 How many times have Sooners players been named Academic All-Americans?

A. 30

7 What is the record attendance at an Oklahoma Sooners game?

A. 88,308

8 When did Bob Stoops have his first season with Oklahoma?

A. 1999

9 When did Bob Stoops become the winningest coach in Sooners history?

A. 2013

10 Where is the Sooners stadium located?

A. Norman, Oklahoma

Key Words

draft: an annual event where the NFL chooses college football players to be new team members

Heisman Memorial Trophy: an annual award given to the college football player who best demonstrates excellence and hard work

landscape: the land features in a specific area

offensive coordinator: a coaching staff member of a gridiron football team who is in charge of the offense

postseason: a sporting event that takes place after the end of the regular season

recruiting: working to enroll someone as a member of an organization

renovate: to improve or expand an older building

rivalries: competitions between different groups or individuals toward the same objective or goal

settlers: people who move to an area where few people have lived before

territory: an area of land controlled by a ruler or state

Index

Bedlam Series 7
Big 12 Conference 5, 10, 11, 19, 22, 23
Blanton, Scott 25
Bradford, Sam 23

Gaylord Family Oklahoma Memorial Stadium 5, 8, 9, 10, 14, 21, 26, 30

Johnson, Lane 23
Jones, Landry 24

Mayfield, Baker 15, 22, 25
McCoy, Gerald 22
McDonald, Tommy 6
Murray, DeMarco 24

National Collegiate Athletic Association (NCAA) 6, 17
National Football League (NFL) 15, 22, 23, 27

Orange Bowl 16, 17

Riley, Lincoln 5, 18, 19, 27

scholarships 15, 22
Sooner Schooner 20, 21
Stoops, Bob 16, 18, 19, 27, 30
Switzer, Barry 19

uniforms 12, 13, 21

Log on to www.av2books.com

AV² by Weigl brings you media enhanced books that support active learning. Go to www.av2books.com, and enter the special code found on page 2 of this book. You will gain access to enriched and enhanced content that supplements and complements this book. Content includes video, audio, weblinks, quizzes, a slideshow, and activities.

AV² Online Navigation

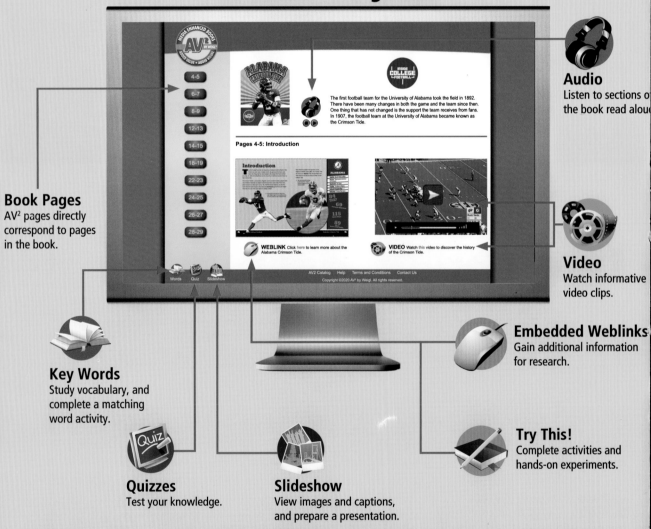

Audio
Listen to sections of the book read aloud.

Video
Watch informative video clips.

Embedded Weblinks
Gain additional information for research.

Try This!
Complete activities and hands-on experiments.

Book Pages
AV² pages directly correspond to pages in the book.

Key Words
Study vocabulary, and complete a matching word activity.

Quizzes
Test your knowledge.

Slideshow
View images and captions, and prepare a presentation.

AV² was built to bridge the gap between print and digital. We encourage you to tell us what you like and what you want to see in the future.

Sign up to be an AV² Ambassador at www.av2books.com/ambassador.